The Little Book of Vegan Poems

EXPLICIT *Vegan* LYRICS

Benjamin Zephaniah

The Little Book of Vegan Poems

ISBN 1-902593-33-2

Library of Congress Cataloguing-in-Publication Data
A catalogue record for this title is available from the
Library of Congress.

British Library Cataloguing-in-Publication Data
A catalogue record for this title is available from the British
Library.

Published by:
AK Press
P O Box 12766
Edinburgh, Scotland
EH 8 9YE

A K Press
P O Box 40682
San Francisco, CA
94140-0682

Cover art, book layout and design by Boff

Warning!

Meat eaters may be offended by these poems

This is not an apology, simply a warning

*

But if you are offended by the strong vegan views in these poems, just think of how vegan children are offended every day, not only by the sight and smells of burning bodies but also by being ridiculed because of their compassion.

Dedication

For the caring, dedicated young vegans of the world. Those vegans who will not stand for any exploitation whatever the species, and who are fighting racism and sexism with all the strength they get from what the earth provides.

Various Definitions Of The Word Vegan

The Collins English Dictionary
A person who refrains from using any animal product whatever for food, clothing or any other purpose.

Oxford English Dictionary (CD-Rom)
A person who on principle abstains from all food of animal origin; a strict vegetarian.

Oxford English Dictionary
A person who does not eat animals or animal products - adj: Using or containing no animal products (shortening of vegetarian).

Websters Dictionary
Not listed

The Hutchinson Encyclopedia (9th Ed.)
A person who eats no food of animal origin, including eggs, milk and honey.

The Cambridge Encyclopedia (1990)
Those who shun all animal foods are known as vegans.

BBC English Dictionary
Someone who does not eat any meat or fish or anything that is produced from an animal such as cheese, butter or milk.

Contents

Vegan Kisses

There's nothing like a vegan kiss
To send you off to sleep at night,
And then another vegan kiss should touch you
When the day is light,
You should get a vegan kiss
When you break your vegan fast,
And then when you go off to school
A vegan kiss will really last.

A vegan kiss will do you good
Because they're healthy I suppose,
A vegan kiss will make you laugh
If you receive one on your nose,
When it comes from your Mom and Dad
Or someone else who really cares
Your vegan kiss is truly yours
But then again it's also theirs.

A vegan kiss that's organic is tasty
And is protein packed,
So if you're being given one
Do not forget to give one back,
A vegan kiss that has no luv
Is only just pretending
So if your kiss does not have luv
Just watch who you're befriending.

9

Every day a vegan poet
Has to have a vegan kiss
And if the poet doesn't get it
The poet knows something's amiss,
A vegan kiss is really special
A vegan kiss is where it's at
A vegan kiss is very luving
For it contains no animal fat.

No true vegan wants to hunt
Vegan cupboards have peace in store,
That's why vegans kiss and hug
Instead of going off to war,
And every time that vegans kiss
A little bit of good is made
And when those vegan lips get dry
Try drinking vegan lemonade.

So humble vegans everywhere
Go tell the world of vegan luv
And to those who don't overstand
Be patient,
Do not push and shove,
Go humble vegan here and there
Speak up, and tell the people this
That luv for every living thing
Is deep within a vegan kiss.

Lost Cow

One day I met a lonely cow
Who told me she was
Lost,
I said to him
'I'll help you friend
My help will bear no cost'
I said
'Now listen
Carefully
I'll tell you what to do,
Go straight ahead,
Turn left,
Turn right
And then you go
Moo moo.'

Mother Cow Speaks

Leave my milk
For my baby
That is ours
And you are crazy,
I think you're just being lazy
Go and drink your own.
My baby needs this milk
And maybe
Your mind is messed up and hazy
All that milk is ours
Leave it be
Leave our milk alone.
We all make milk
For our
Own kind
That is nature's plan
You'll find,
So leave that milk
For my baby
If you would be
So kind.

Vegan Steven

There was a young vegan
Called Steven,
Who just would not kill for no reason,
This kid would not eat
No cheese or no meat
And he hated the foxhunting season.

Pride

I've got no bodies inside me
All of me is me,
I will not eat no body else
So I am what you see.
I do not plan to eat young sheep
I will not eat a hen,
I'm so proud of what I am
I must say once again.
I've got no bodies inside me
All of me is me,
I will not eat no body else
So I am what you see.

We People Too

I have dreams of summer days
Of running freely on the lawn
I luv a lazy Sunday morn
Like many others do.
I luv my family always
I luv clear water in a stream
Oh yes I cry and yes I dream
We dogs are people too.

And I dear folk am small and great
My friends call me the mighty Bruce
I luv to drink pure orange juice
Like many others do.
I hope you all appreciate
We give you all a helping hand
When me and my friends turn the land
We worms are people too.

When I have time I luv sightseeing
You may not want to see my face
But you and me must share a space
Like many others do.
Please think of me dear human being
It seems that I'm always in need
I have a family to feed
We mice are people too.

They say we're really dangerous
But we too like to feel and touch
And we like music very much
Like many others do.
Most of us are not poisonous
I have a little lovely face
I move around with style and grace
We snakes are people too.

I don't mind if you stand and stare
But know that I have luv no end
And my young ones I will defend
Like many others do.
When you see me in the air
Remember that I know the worth
Of all us who share the earth
We birds are people too.

I need fresh air and exercise
I need to safely cross the road,
I carry such a heavy load
Like many others do.
Don't only judge me by my size
Ask any veterinarian
I'm just a vegetarian
We cows are people too.

Water runs straight off my smooth back
And I hold my head high with pride
I like my children at my side

Like many others do.
I don't care if you're white or black
If you like land or air or sea
I want to see more unity
We ducks are people too.

I think living is so cool
And what I really like the most
Is kiss chase and I luv brown toast
Like many others do.
I hang around in a big skool
I only need a little sleep
I like thinking really deep
We fish are people too.

I luv the cows I love the trees
And I would rather you not smoke
For if you smoke then I would choke
Like many others do.
I beg you not to squash me please
I do not want to cause you harm
I simply want you to stay calm
We flies are people too.

My name is Thomas Tippy Tops
Billy is not my name
I've learnt to live with fame
Like many others do.
I once was on Top Of The Pops
On TV I sang loud

My parents were so proud
We goats are people too.

I luv to walk among the fern
I'm thankful for each night and day
I really luv to holiday
Like many others do.
I've read the books and my concern
Is why do we always look bad
My friends don't think I'm raving mad
We wolves are people too.

A lovely garden makes me smile
A good joke makes me croak
One day I want to own a boat
Like many others do.
I'd luv to see the river Nile
I'd luv my own sandcastle
I really want to travel
We frogs are people too.

Please do not call me horrid names
Think of me as a brother
I'm quite nice you'll discover
Like many others do.
If you're my friend then call me James
I'll be your friend forever more
I'll be the one that you adore
We pigs are people too.

We really need this planet
And we want you to be aware
We just don't have one spare
Not any of us do.

We dogs, we goats
We mice, we snakes
Even we worms
Are really great,
We birds, we cows
We ducks, we frogs
Are just trying to do our jobs
We wolves, we fish
We pigs, we flies
Could really open up your eyes
And all we want to say to you
Is that
We all are people too.

Me Girlfriend

Me girlfriend is a Vegan
Me girlfriend is a Vegan
She nibbles at me Carrots
I nibble at her Carrots
She's crabbing up me Plantain
I'm crabbing up her Plantain
She's always at me Apples
I'm always at her Apples.

Me girlfriend is a Vegan
Me girlfriend is a Vegan
She's gotta lotta Melon
I too hav plenty Melon
She touches up me Turnips
Then I touch up her Turnips
She juices me Mangoes
I luv to juice her Mangoes.

Me girlfriend is a Vegan
Me girlfriend is a Vegan
We both really like Rice
We both really like Rice
She plays wid me Pears
She plays wid me Pears
An we both feel nice
Yes we both feel nice.

Fight For Your Bite Rights

If the young vegan kids of our nation
Are at school and can't get vegan bites,
Then the school staff need food education
Because safe food are one of our rights.

Anti-Slavery Movements

Some people say
Animal liberators are not
Working in the best interest of animals
But I've never seen liberated animals
Protest by going back to their place
Of captivity.
But then again
I've never heard of any liberated slaves
Begging for more humiliation
Or voting for slavery.

Animals vote with their feet
Or their wings
Or their fins.

Mr Money

I've got money in my pocket
But I cannot buy clean air,
And I am worried sick about
All the pollution everywhere.

I've got money in my pocket
But I cannot save the forest,
And I cannot buy a government
That's very, very honest.

There is money in my pocket
For my money I give thanks,
I am told the poor have no food
And no money in their banks.

Yes there's money in my pocket
But I cannot live forever,
And when the days are cloudy
Money cannot change the weather.

I've got lots of pounds and lots of pence
But when the shops are closed
There's no one to impress
And my emotions are exposed.

I've got money deals all over
I may also have a friend

Instead of plastic smiling people
Who do nothing but pretend.

I know money people from abroad
Who love me for my money,
And I am trying very hard
To try and love somebody.

I have the latest, fastest car
To show others my wealth,
This car can take me far
But it can't help me face myself.

I've got money in my pocket
What does all this money mean,
If I cannot respect others?
I am just a human being.

I've got money in my pocket
But I can't find any love,
And I still don't know the secrets
Of the heavens up above.

Nature Trail

At the bottom of my garden
There's a hedgehog and a frog
And a lot of creepy-crawlies
Living underneath a log,
There's a baby daddy long legs
And an easy-going snail
And a family of woodlice
All are on my nature trail.

There are caterpillars waiting
For their time to come to fly,
There are worms turning the earth over
As ladybirds fly by,
Birds will visit, cats will visit
But they always choose their time
And I've even seen a fox visit
This wild garden of mine.

Squirrels come to nick my nuts
And busy bees come buzzing
And when the night time comes
Sometimes some dragonflies come humming,
My garden mice are very shy
And I've seen bats that growl
And in my garden I have seen
A very wise old owl.

My garden is a lively place
There's always something happening,
There's this constant search for food
And then there's all that flowering,
When you have a garden
You will never be alone
And I believe we all deserve
A garden of our own.

Peace Eats

There's no vegan who is the greatest
Because all you vegans are great,
Just like the peace dove
You symbolise love,
And there is no death on your plate.

Remember I Never Forget

I'm an elephant
I never forget,
I've wandered for miles
And I've not got lost yet,
I remember all the birds
That free ride on my head
I remember each time that I sleep in a bed.

I'm an elephant
I never forget,
I can recall each visit
I've made to the vet,
I remember my birth
And I know where I am from
I remember first seeing my Dad and my Mom.

I'm an elephant
I never forget,
I have a toy bath
And I have a train set,
I have a computer with a memory
But it cannot remember a thing without me.

I'm an elephant
Please don't get upset,
But I once had a human
I kept as a pet,

I remember his bad jokes
His charm and his style,
But he ran away with a cute crocodile.

I'm an elephant
I never forget,
I once made a trip
In a big jumbo jet,
The passengers were quite excited to see
A jumbo with a jumbo of a pilot like me.

I'm an elephant
I never forget,
I know everybody
That I've ever met,
I know every question
In every quiz,
My bottom is big
But I know where it is.

Eat Your Words

I am a veggie table
A table made of veg,
There's so much fruit upon me
All living on the edge,
Life is hard
But so are plates
And tea can be quite hot,
And vegetarian poets
Make me nervous quite a lot.

Gender Pretender

I know a dog that is a girl
But she thinks she's a boy,
I wonder where he gets his brains
Because he is a toy,
All this may sound confusing
But trust me I am an expert,
I know this doggy is a teddy bear
Because of his skirt.

The Banana Drama

I dream of banana chips
And a tree that will grow jelly,
I dream of having lots of
Banana jelly
In my belly,
I'm as happy as a hippy
And for sure I have no doubts
About the energy and goodness
You get from bananas
And sprouts.

I've never had a dream
To be a prince, a king or queen,
But each day I think that I
Should eat
Things that are yellow or green,
I'm crazy about
Ackee,
Broccoli,
And I've started to think
That I'm slowly falling in love with
The colour known as pink.

I know that I am going bananas
And I know that I like being this way,
Now I'm going off to school in my pyjamas

And I don't care what my teacher has to say.

I've been eating lots of peas,
And I like them.
No I love them.
Yesterday I had
A great big piece of yam,
And tonight I'm going to
Find some trees and hug them,
Yes I'll hug them,
That's the kind of rasta poet
That I am.
And then I'm going to
Get me a chapatti,
And I'm going to share it
With a friendly cat,
And if I cannot find
The cat that sat upon the mat
Well I'll just share it with
My friend call bit the bat.

I know that I am going bananas
And I know that I like being this way,
Now I'm going off to school in my pyjamas
And I don't care what my teacher has to say.

Now the time has come
To go and do some learning,
And I'm really looking forward
To the maths,

I'm looking forward to the time
The bell rings,
Because I want to do some
Nutty arts and crafts,
On the way to school I saw
No people staring,
I was much too busy talking
With the birds,
But then when I saw
What my teacher was wearing
For some strange reason
I was lost for words.

I think my teacher has gone bananas
And it seems to me that he's happy that way,
And my teacher's dressed in lovely pink pyjamas
And he don't care what other teachers say,
It's so good to know that others go bananas
Maybe we should live together in the jungle,
But we'll need to take a spare pair of pyjamas
If we want to make some pink banana crumble.

Birdland

I can remember
The first time I flew.
The thrill of the take off
The joy of the lift
The victory over gravity.
I so enjoyed
Cruising over clouds,
I so enjoyed
Looking out for angels,
How I enjoyed
Looking down
On the tiny people below
And wondering
If they were looking up at me
And wondering.

The birds were cool.
Flying is wonderful
And landing is exciting.
Yes I can remember
The first time I flew.
It was great.
I still fly
Every now and then
But now I use aeroplanes.

No Pain, No Shame

I do like a good veggie burger
The reasons just couldn't be clearer,
They're full of the best
And unlike the rest
They do not involve any murder.

Trees Please

Leave de trees please
Cause de trees
Work wid de breeze
To put all living tings at ease,
So leave de trees please.

Yu see
Down in Somerset, England,
I know a tree
Dat is one thousand
An five hundred years old.
Dat is a wise tree
Dat is a tree I need
To talk to,
Dat is a tree
We animals should listen to.

For millions of animals
Trees are a home,
Trees can help shelter yu home,
So leave de trees alone.
Trees mek oxygen
Let me say dat again
Trees mek oxygen
So mek a tree yu fren

Leave de trees please

Cause de trees
Work wid de breeze
To put all living tings at ease,
An they help de birds an bees
Old an wise are all of these,
So leave de trees please
Juss
Leave de trees please.

Coconuts Must

Coconuts must
Grow up
Before dem
Cum
DOWN.

Coconuts must
Be green
Before dem
Turn
BROWN.

Coconuts must
Break
Before you
Can
DRINK.

Coconuts must
Go to school
Before they
Can
THINK.

Vegan Steven's Vegan Clothes

Remember that vegan called Steven
Yes he would not kill for no reason,
Well I saw him today
Wearing nothing I say
But some cabbage leaves
With a few peas on.

Bloody Food

We don't want yu bloody food,
Sold wid yu bloody lies,
Most of it is simply blood
Dat is under a disguise.

We don't want yu bloody food,
Dat's no recipe fe luv,
Dat's a recipe from murder,
What de hell yu tinking of?

We don't want yu bloody food,
Give we vegetables dat fresh
We don't want to eat ded life
We don't want to bite at flesh.

We don't want yu bloody food,
Cause we tink we all are equal,
So let's look at it honestly
In truth
You're really eating people.

Websites

AK's catalogue can be browsed and ordered from:
http://www.akuk.com

For those who would find an American catalogue more useful, go to:
http://www.akpress.org

More information about Benjamin Zephaniah can be found at:
http://www.oneworld.org/zephaniah/
and
http://www.oneworld.org/yes/benjamin/

Useful Organisations

The Vegan Society

Donald Watson House,
7 Battle Road,
St. Leonards-on-Sea,
East Sussex TN37 7AA
Tel: 01424 427393
Web site: http://www.vegansociety.com

VIVA! (Vegetarians International Voice for Animals)

12 Queen Square,
Brighton,
East Sussex BN1 3FD
Tel: 01273 777688

NAVS (National Anti-Vivisection Society)

261 Goldhawk Road,
London W12 9PE
Tel: 0181 846 9777

Animal Aid Youth Group

The Old Chapel,
Bradford Street,
Tonbridge,
Kent TN9 1AW
Tel: 01732 366533
Web site: http://www.animalaid.org.uk

Hillside Animal Sanctuary

Hall Lane,
Frettenham,
Norwich NR12 7LT
Tel: 01603 891227

Dr Hadwen Trust For Humane Research

22 Bancroft,
Hitchin,
Hertfordshire SG5 1JW
Web site: http://www.envirolink.org/DrHT/index.html

Children Are Unbeatable (against corporal punishment)

77 Holloway Road,
London N7 8JZ
Tel: 0171 700 0627

Childline

Tel: 0800 1111

Message Home (contact your loved ones if you are away from home)

Tel: 0500 700 740

About Benjamin Zephaniah

Dr Benjamin Obadiah Iqbal Zephaniah was born in Birmingham in 1958. He spent some of his early years in Jamaica where he absorbed much of the island culture which was later to have a dramatic affect on his work. At the age of 12 he was taken out of comprehensive school and sent to an approved school on the grounds that he was uncontrollable, rebellious and as the teacher put it, "a born failure". Ironically Benjamin now spends a large amount of his time visiting schools, youth clubs, prisons, universities and teacher training centres. By the time he was 15 he developed a strong following in his home town of Handsworth where he had a reputation for speaking on local and international issues.

He came to London aged 22 and his first book *Pen Rhythm* (Page One Books) was published soon after. Although highly popular within the Afro-Caribbean and Asian community he soon sought a wider, mainstream audience. *The Dread Affair* (Arena), his second published book, caused a stir because of its condemnation of the institutions of Law and Order and his unorthodox use of the English language. He has since published *Inna Liverpool* (Africa Arts Collective) and *Rasta Time in Palestine*, which is part poetry, part travelogue account of his journey through the occupied territories. *City Psalms*, published by Bloodaxe Books, showcases his versatility as he works with the page in mind, as opposed to the other books of performance poetry. This was followed by *Propa Propaganda* (Bloodaxe) and *School's Out* (AK Press) where he has collected the 'poems dat are bad for you, the rejects. My Favourites' together specially with kids in mind. His first novel, *Face*, has recently been published by Bloomsbury, and *Wicked World* (Penguin), a new book of poems for children, is also newly published.

Benjamin has toured Europe, Canada, USA, India and the Caribbean amongst other places. He caused considerable controversy when he was short listed for the post of Creative Artist in Residence at Cambridge University and later short listed to become Professor of Poetry at Oxford University. Many people believed that he was treated very unfairly by the press, most of all, it seems, the people of Liverpool who went on to lobby their local Arts Council to invite Benjamin to work in their City alongside interested parties. He went on to spend two years as Writer-in-Residence in Liverpool for the City with the Africa Arts Collective, time which was spent mainly working with young people and students.

One of the first documentaries ever shown on Channel 4 was about Benjamin's work which was followed by an updated documentary in November 1987 and since then both programmes have been repeated. Over the years he has appeared on chat shows, music and poetry programmes as well as political debates. He has also appeared in some films, the Comic Strip *Didn't You Kill My Brother?* with Alexei Sayle and *Farendg* where he played the part of Moses. This film was shot in Ethiopia and was shown at Cannes Film Festival 1990. At the end of 1991 the BBC produced Benjamin's first television play *Dread Poets Society*; he co-wrote and played himself in the play in which he is confronted by Mary Shelley, Bysshe Shelley, Lord Byron and Keats.

His records are *Big Boys Don't Make Girls Cry*, *Free South Africa*, which was recorded with The Wailers, *Dub Ranting, Rasta*, the album and *Us an Dem* released in June 1990 on the Island/Mango label. The year 1992 saw the release of *Crisis* by Workers Playtime, and the Benjamin Zephaniah Band on tour. More recently, cassettes of his performance poetry have been produced - *Overstanding* and *Radical Rapping* - as well as a CD called *Reggae Head* (57 Productions).

His plays are *Playing the Right Tune* (Theatre East), *Job Rocking* (Riverside Studios), *Hurricane Dub* (BBC Radio), *Streetwise* (Temba) and *Delirium* (Union Dance Company) and *The Trial of Mickey Tekka* for the Hay-on-Wye Literature Festival. *Hurricane Dub* was published as one of the winners in the BBC's Young Playwrights Festival 1988.

He is Chairperson of the Hackney Empire Theatre and Umoja Housing Co-op, Patron of the Irie Dance Company, Market Nursery-Hackney, Newham Young People's Theatre Scheme, the Chinese Women's Refuge Group, Music Works-Bristol, Newcastle One Work Association and president of Penrose (self-help housing organisation for ex-prisoners), patron of VIVA (animal welfare group) and of the Vegan Society.

Benjamin's work goes hand in hand with his interest in politics which grew out of his concern for people as opposed to an academic interest. He is well known for his views on British issues but is also working with and meeting people from Palestine, South Africa, East Timor, Ethiopia, Kurdistan, Pakistan, Sri Lanka, Guyana, Chile and Nicaragua. On two occasions his work has been quoted in the House of Commons! Lately he has been seen presenting TV programmes on the Arts, Politics and Children's TV, as well as the acclaimed *Passport to Liverpool* radio documentary produced by Radio 4.

All the following titles are available by mail order from AK Distribution

Please add 10% of the total cost of your order for post and packaging and make cheques, postal orders or IMO's payable to AK Distribution

All orders to: PO Box 12766 Edinburgh, Scotland EH8 9YE

We can also accept credit card orders by telephone on 0131 555 5165, by fax on 0131 555 5215, or by e mail: orders@akedin.demon.co.uk

If you would like to receive the latest AK catalogue featuring thousands of radical books, magazines, pamphlets and comics please send a large SAE to the above PO Box address

Resources

Animal Ingredients A to Z
AK Press   1 873176 59 7   £4.95

This easy-to-use, concise reference for vegans, vegetarians, the health-conscious, and curious alike, documents thousands of animal and animal derived ingredients.

Contents include an extensive chapter on vegan nutrition; over 150 listings complete with explanations and alternatives; over 200 beers, wines, and information on the ever confusing world of cider; alphabetical listings of animal derived ingredients and ingredients that can sometimes be animal derived; a thorough resource guide.

Drawn from such sources as PETA, the Vegan Society and manufacturers themselves, cross-checked and referenced, this handy book helps to de-mystify concerns over postage stamps, chewing gum, teas and maple syrup.

With over 2000 listings in all, this is the most comprehensive guide
available for those concerned with what they purchase, and consume.

"The purpose of this book isn't to preach about why you shouldn't eat
animals and how animals are tortured because of societies consumption
of them. It has been compiled as a working reference for those who are
most likely vegan, and who wonder if Dihydroxyethyl Soyamine
Dioleate in their favorite potato chips is vegan (which it isn't)...." [from
the introduction]

**Cooking with PETA: Great Vegan Recipes for a Compassionate
Kitchen**
ISBN: 1 57067 0 447   £11.99

One of the cornerstones of the People For the Ethical Treatment of
Animals advocacy is the use of substitutes for meat, dairy, eggs and
honey as well as other foods derived from animals. This book shows
how to prepare delicious meals without imposing on other species of the
planet.

**Vegan Vittles: A Collection of Recipes Inspired by the Critters of
Farm Sanctuary**
ISBN: 1 57067 0 250   £9.99

Farm Sanctuary is the largest sanctuary for victims of food animal pro-
duction in the U.S. Its founders have teamed up with top vegan cook-
ery author Joanne Stepaniak to present a plethora of delicious dishes.
There is a section on nutritional information, and a chapter on Veganism
and what to substitute for eggs, milk and dairy products.

Recommended Reading

School's Out: Poems Not For School
Benjamin Zephaniah
187317649X   £3.95

A classic collection of poetry from the internationally acclaimed Rasta poet. 34 'children's' poems which their parents will appreciate too. Includes 'Peace Increase', 'De Rich Gettin Rich', 'Recession', 'It's Work', 'Revolutions' and 'A Marriage Of Minds' amongst others.

Shattered
Spot the Poet (Steve Pottinger)
1873176589   £4.95

Shattered is a collection of work by one of Britain's best performance poets. Spot's poetry is accessible, but never patronising to its audience or its subjects. Clearly furious about the state of the nation, this is no frail call to arms or ideological polemic. Rather, he recognises life as it is lived and as he sees others live it, both bitter and sweet and never as you expect it. His work is sensitive and perceptive, but it pulls no punches. While some of these (true) stories will have you close to tears, others will make you laugh. A real gem.

Kissing it All
Steve Pottinger
1873176325   £4.95

The second awe inspiring volume of verse from the poet previously known as Spot. Witty, sad, gloriously human. A book to convert all those friends that insist they don't like poetry.

Rage and Reason - **The ultimate animal rights revenge novel**
Michael Tobias   1 873176 56 2   £7.95

"Not a single statement in the newspapers or magazines ever came out in support of what he was doing. The condemnation from animal groups was unanimous. Felham was nothing more than a terrorist. How could he continue to believe in his war, against such universal condemnation?"

Michael Tobias' latest work of fiction is a shocking, breath-stopping political thriller which tracks the fury of an outraged ex-Special Forces veteran who turns to violent retribution in defense of the earth and its fauna.

Rage and Reason is an unstoppable rollercoaster of action which explodes across four continents

Rage and Reason is as vivid a portrayal of the horrors of vivisection and the meat industry as Upton Sinclair's classic 'The Jungle'

"Who hasn't raged at injustice? Or fantasized about snuffing out those who knowingly kill all that is good? Should it matter whether the victims are black or white, innocent children, helpless animals, streams, or forests? Michael Tobias gives life to such desperate thoughts, melding morality with high adventure, and action with anguish. A terrific story, told from the heart, its soul rich with knowledge. Some people and corporations should lose sleep wondering if RAGE & REASON will ever become a real life thriller for them."

(Ingrid E. Newkirk, President, PETA -People For The Ethical Treatment Of Animals)

*